Given to Love

GIVEN TO LOVE

CHERYL STASINOWSKY

WORD SCRIBE

GIVEN TO LOVE
Copyright © 2015 by Cheryl Stasinowsky

All rights reserved. No part of this book may be reproduced, stored in a retrieval system, or transmitted in any form or by any means-electronic, mechanical, photocopy, recording, or otherwise-without prior written permission of the copyright owner, except by a reviewer who wishes to quote brief passages in connection with a review for inclusion in a magazine, website, newspaper, podcast, or broadcast. Cheryl Stasinowsky does not capitalize the name of satan or any reference to the devil.

All Scripture quotations, unless otherwise indicated, are taken from the New King James Version of the Bible. Copyright © 1982 by Thomas Nelson, Inc.

Cover photo of Cheryl by Sarah Mueller.

Interior design and cover design provided by www.truenorthpublish.com.

Published by WordScribe.

ISBN: 978-0692485514

For Worldwide Distribution. Published in the United States of America.

Dedications

My Generations

I dedicate this book to my children and to their children, and to generations that I will never see or get to talk to. I am talking to you through this book. I am given to love for you! May my love today reach through time and touch you. I am praying for you and I love you!!

Monique and Mike

I dedicate this book to you both...You are true people given to love. You are both my heros. May God richly bless you and your amazing girls. I love you!!

Rylee Hope

I dedicate this book to you. You fulfilled your purpose in life. Because of you, I have gotten to meet your mom, grandma and grandpa, and your life is changing generations. Love is winning little one. Tell Jesus hi and give Him a hug!

My Family

I am "Given to Love" them

Table of Contents

Acknowledgements
Endorsements
Introduction

Chapter 1: We Get Back Up 23
Chapter 2: But Have Not Love 29
Chapter 3: Love Is 33
Chapter 4: His Top 10 39
Chapter 5: Love Yourself 51
Chapter 6: Heart to Heart 57
Chapter 7: Are You Persuaded? 63
Chapter 8: For God So Loved 67
Chapter 9: Given to Love 71
Chapter 10: Truth in Love 75
Chapter 11: Let Them Be 81
Chapter 12: Rylee Hope 85
Chapter 13: Say "Thank-You!" 93
Chapter 14: Hand It Over 97
Chapter 15: A Hug 101
Chapter 16: His Commandment 105
Chapter 17: So Love Is 109

About the Author
More Titles by Cheryl Stasinowsky

Acknowledgements

Father, Son, and Holy Spirit

Thank You for continuing to teach me about Your love for me, so that I am able to give love to the world around me. I do not ever want to stop learning and being given to love! I love You!!

Mom

Determined love has brought us to a relationship that we both longed for and dreamed of. I love you and thank you for birthing me and showing me unconditional love. I love you, mom!!

Wally

You have loved me well. You believe in me and have supported me. You have worked while allowing me to write. You have taken care of me and read each part of this book as it was being developed. You listened. You read. You listened and you read.
Thank you and I love you!!

Amber, Daniel, and Jordan

I love living life with you! You each continue to teach me more and more about love. I promise to love you the best that I can. I promise to continue to love God and be given to His love so that I can be given to love you better! How I love you!!

Jean

Yet again, you have said, "Yes", to editing another one of my books. Your willing heart to read and re-read amaze me. You are a pleasure to be corrected by. This is a better book because of you.
May the Lord richly bless you!!

Brian

Another book! You have been such a blessing to me. I love how you listen and create and are always open to my vision for the books we bring to completion together. Thank you! You make this possible. May the Lord richly bless you and your family!!

Friends and Readers

Without you, this book would have no point or purpose. I hope you will feel as if I am speaking one on one with you. I greatly appreciate you. Thank you for your encouragement and recommendations to your friends. Thank you for the pictures of highlighted pages, for the private notes of how you are growing closer to the Lord, and just for loving Jesus! With my arms open wide I say, "THANK YOU!!"

Endorsements

Given to Love is an invitation into the fierce love of God. In today's culture where love, or better yet, the idea of love, has become somewhat confusing for most people, Cheryl Stasinowsky offers bold and timely wisdom for those who desire a greater and deeper understanding of authentic love. A journey into the story of God and through her own personal discoveries, Given to Love will both equip and empower you to love yourself, to love others, and to love God like never before. It's time to learn what love truly is.

Nathan Edwardson, Lead Pastor
The Stirring, California

I really appreciated Cheryl's insights and perspective on the very broad topic of love. There is so much that could be said, so many paths to travel down while exploring the topic of love. Cheryl's writing is very practical, pointed, and personal. Her thoughts and experiences as she meditated and reflected on Scripture were full of life, conviction and depth. It felt a bit like being invited into her own personal conversation with the Lord regarding His word and what He had to say about being given to love. I found myself returning to the chapter on 1 Corinthians 13. After reading through it I had a tremendous desire to sit down and work myself through 1 Corinthians 13, asking myself some of the questions Cheryl encouraged us as readers to ask. I felt the Holy Spirit prompting me to consider the significant relationships in my life through the lens of 1 Corinthians 13. The simplicity and depth that Cheryl writes with makes reading her books on weighty topics such as love and forgiveness easy to read, but with so much to return to and ponder on. Her writing inspires me to have my own conversations with the Lord; to visit His Word and invite the Holy Spirit to move through the places of my heart and call me into deeper ways of being given to love.

Amy Bailey, California

Having read "Given to Forgive", Cheryl's previous book, and the tremendous life transformation that occurred within my relationship with the Lord, I was excited to read "Given to Love". Cheryl has such a gift as an author, wife, mother, and a true believer and follower of the Lord. "Given To Love", gave me the opportunity to really take a deeper look at what "love" truly meant to me.

It is a word we all say and use, but do we truly ever stop and consider just what we are saying? As I read this book, and meditated on the words, and scripture that Cheryl references, I truly felt the presence of the Spirit within me, and in my heart, and what the Lord wanted me to understand as the true meaning of love. Cheryl's love and awareness of the Lord in her life, shares first hand through her life, just how we can love as the Lord loves each of us, how we can learn the true meaning of love, and how we should truly learn to love as does the Lord. Cheryl gives excellent scripture references, and I was truly challenged to reach deep down inside myself, and think if I was truly using the word "love" as it is intended to be used or just saying it without thinking of love's true meaning. I've got a better understanding of my meaning and use of love after reading, Given to Love.

Cheryl writes as if she is sitting right in front of me, face to face, asking me and giving me true life and scripture examples of how, as Christians, we should and can love like the Lord. I cannot express how much I encourage everyone to read this book, especially if you have read "Given To Forgive"; this book will helped complete my transformation into the person that I wanted to become. I have found a favorite author in the way Cheryl writes about her own personal struggles and victories that all of us face daily in our own lives as spouses, parents, and believers and followers of Christ. I feel that with all the chaos going on in the world today, if we all read this book, and truly learned to love as the Lord loves, we could start getting back to the way we are intended to live by the Word, loving each other. I'm excited to see how the Lord is talking to Cheryl as she starts writing the next book on how to become better followers of Christ!

Timothy Lopez, Oklahoma

Love--always do what is in the other person's best interest regardless of how you feel about the situation at the time. This is love; this is Cheryl--given to love, even to willingly share herself and her personal learning experiences in order to teach others to learn to be given to love. Whether it is for yourself, or to help another, "Given to Love" is a very excellent teaching tool, for there is not a person alive who does not need to learn to be more loving and to give more love. Good work, Cheryl, thanks.

Jean Hudak Kashella, Pennsylvania

Given to Love challenges us to reevaluate and transform the way we love and receive love in a very practical way. With an especially moving, in depth, look at the Ten Commandments and Psalm 139, we are encouraged to push the boundaries of where we believe love begins and ends. If you desire deeper revelation and transformation, this book is for you. You will never love the same again.

Janessa Yarnell, aspiring missionary and Rylee Hope's mama, California

In preparation, prior to Cheryl approaching me regarding her new book, the Father had me in 1 Corinthians 13 for a few weeks. And I have been quickened to many things being done in the body of Christ in the name of the advancement of the Kingdom of God, and yet, they are lacking in power because they are lacking in love. In all the things I have seen as a Seer I have seen that God is LOVE. Nothing He does is separate of this. Acts 17:28 says, "for in Him we live and move and have our being," For us to live and move in Him we must live and move in love. We must give ourselves to love, and in this process we see that we are, in fact, given to love.

As I read through Cheryl's book Given to Love I found myself reflecting on situations where I didn't act in love, and pondered a different outcome if I had. I found myself recognizing treasures strategically placed in my life to teach me how to love and how to be given to love. I spent priceless time before the Father as I was deeply entrenched in Cheryl's words. And the question that kept coming to my mind was this, "What have we gained if we love when it's easy?" For anyone can do that. But what is of eternal worth is being given to love in situations where it is hard to love, when our humanness is pushed beyond its capabilities and we find ourselves acting more out of our spiritual side than our natural side. It is in the reaching beyond ourselves in such situations that we can truly see the heart of God. We, then and only then, can advance His kingdom and experience heaven on earth. Good job Cheryl and God bless you and all who read this book.

Erica Christopher, Seer, Author and Speaker
The Making of a Seer: A personal journey into the spiritual realms
www.ericachristopher.com

Introduction

A Heart Impacted by Love

Oh Lord God, nothing is impossible for You! I love Your word. The more You open it up to me, the more I love it. You gave us Your word to teach us about Your love, to show us Your love, to show us You and who You are to us and for us. You gave us Your word for love and in love. You loved us so much that You gave Your only begotten Son to come and walk on this earth to show us how love walks among the challenges of life. You showed us what love looks like, feels like, sounds like, and is like. You want us to know what You created us to do. You gave us Your word so we will understand Your Faithfulness, Your Strength, Your Determination, Your Love, Mercy, and Grace.

You want us to know that You are love. You are a love that the world does not understand. The world tried to define love, but You are love. You created us to love. You have given us to the world around us to love, just as You first gave Jesus out of love. I know that I cannot give what I do not have. My love has failed so many times in life.

I grew up with a distorted view of love from family, movies, television, failed friendships, people saying they love me and then turning on me the next moment. I learned not to trust love or words from the world, and so You met me right where I was and began teaching me what Your love for me looked like. As I read Your word, You showed me love. It was as if one verse unlocked another. I do not know how You do that, but I know You do.

You have put this book together. You have prepared each writing through my own struggles and challenges of life when I met Your love in them. When I was confronted by people, You taught me how to choose love. When I wanted to fight, You gave me the weapon of love. When I was disappointed, You taught me how to stand back up because of Your love for me. You taught me how to love with my words, with my actions, with my thoughts, with how I listen and give. You taught me love from observation, from revelation, and from a hug. You taught me how to speak truth in love and not avoid it. You helped me love myself so I could love others. You would lead me to a section of Your word and change the lenses on my glasses to view it from the perspective of love. You captivated me with Your love. I love Your unshakable, steadfast, unfailing, never-ending love for me, with me, and through me. I, too, join the list of people persuaded that nothing can separate us from Your love for us.

Your love casts out fear! Your love brings security and comfort! Your love listens! Your love helps and strengthens! Your love is wisdom! The more I discover about Your love through life's challenges, the more I am able to be given to it. I am given to love You! I am given to love because of You! It is only possible with You!

You have been writing this book inside of me for my entire life. You have developed it within me. Oh Lord, may this book richly bless others. May it open eyes to see and ears to hear. May hearts and minds be opened to Your love in a new and fresh way. May this book release encounters with Your love, as I have encountered Your love. May hearts be healed. May love be restored. May perspectives be adjusted and may relationships be healthy. May love be chosen first over being right. May this book bring the possibility of transformed and renewed minds to love as 1 Corinthians 13:4-8. May this book be a cold drink in the desert. May this book open up Your word in ways that are deep and enriching. May the stories, situations, and revelations in this book reach the intended hearts and minds in this world You have purposed for them to reach. May we be a generation given to love so that the next generation will be given to love. May pride be halted with love! May love win! May Your eyes go to and fro across this earth and see Your people Given to love! I love You and thank You! Amen!!

This is my heart and prayer for this book. It is not going to be what you think it is going to be. This is not a book on love as the world sees and shows love. This is a book on my journey through discovering how to love from His word working in and through me. I have purposed to try to put on His word and live love. I am still learning, but what I have learned, I give. It has not been easy. It has not happened overnight. It has been tested and tried and has hurt a lot. I have submitted to Him in difficult situations and have chosen to walk as He showed and not how my flesh wanted to respond. I would encourage you to spend some time in this book. Allow it to teach you and open up your heart. Have your journal ready. Get a highlighter; turn on some worship music. Get away with God, and may you truly encounter the love of God in a new and fresh way.

While I was writing this book, I was listening to two albums, "I Will Not Be Shaken" by Bethel Music and "You Make Me Brave" by Bethel Music. I had the thought awhile back to let readers know what I was listening to as I wrote. I felt like it would give a greater experience with the Holy Spirit...

Share this book with family and friends...not my will be done, but His! May we love as He loves one moment at a time...Enjoy!!

CHAPTER 1
We Get Back Up

Recently, as I sat and looked at our wedding picture, I thought, what do a nineteen year old and a twenty year old know about marriage? The truth is...nothing, but we do not know what we do not know. So, we think we are ready. We believe we have the love to have an amazing life. We do and say all the right things. We spend hours talking and planning. But really, what did we know about marriage, other than the marriages we had experienced with our parents and felt we witnessed in those around us. But what did we know about marriage? I look back now and wonder what in the world were we thinking...

So, here I am today, thirty-three years later, looking at all the years and moments that are in between as we got up close and personal in learning about love and marriage, and finding out all we did not know. People can look at our lives and the pictures and think it has been this perfect life, but what does perfect look like anyway? Has it been easy? Absolutely not! Have we fought and argued? Absolutely yes! What do you think you get when you put two strong-willed-and-determined people together? This is the true meaning of iron sharpening iron. What has kept this marriage together when many others are falling apart? Sometimes, besides the grace of God, it has been sheer determination not to give up and quit. We made vows to each other not to give up and this is where the strong-willed-and-determined people like us dig in; we were given to love.

Over the years, we have had amazing moments, success, laughter, and great memories. We have been knocked down to the point of sitting on the bathroom floor looking at each other and saying that we have no idea how to move forward in this marriage. We have just cried and cried at our mistakes and words and actions we have chosen. But God, who made us, made us determined, and He has remained with us from that first day when we included Him in our vows. I believe He has kept us together. When our mouths were speaking that we wanted to quit, He, somehow, picked us both back up and told us to try again and again and again. When we wanted to quit being given, He continued to be given to love for us, with us, and in us...

We have experienced deep moments of death that changed us. We have experienced wealth and financial struggle. We have experienced fear, loss, hurt, and all the things everyone else in the world experiences, but we are determined. We are determined to discover this thing called marriage and love and make it work. We have prayed and hoped and dreamed. We have hurt each other, and I have controlled far more than I should have. We were learning how to be given to love...

A while back, I was sitting with the Lord complaining about my husband, Wally. Yes, I fight being critical and everything else. So, as I was complaining, the Lord told me that everything I was complaining about, I created. Over the years, my words and actions have contributed to who he is today. So, if I wanted him to change, I had to change first. Yikes, that was not what I wanted to hear. I wanted God to agree with me. He showed me I had dug in my heels and was determined to change when he changed, but the fact was...I needed to change first. Given to love includes changing to love...

I began working on me. I started forgiving him every day. Not to his face, but in my time with the Lord, I would purpose to forgive him and ask the Lord to forgive him, and then ask the Lord to forgive me, and I forgave myself. I also began reading and studying 1 Corinthians 13, and as I saw how I was the clanging cymbal, I began to pray and make this chapter my prayer guide and hearts cry to the Lord. I took that determined individual inside of me and made her purpose to change the way He showed me to change. I gave Him full permission to work on me. I got my eyes and energy off of trying to change Wally and put it into changing me. I quit blaming and took responsibility for my part. Given to love is forgiving and taking responsibility for myself...

I learned that being still and knowing that He is God meant that I needed to be still with my mouth. I was amazed as I started to do this, as I would hear my thoughts of what

I would have said, and it was not good. Those little digs and comments that break down the other person are not a joke to them. Yes, we can convince ourselves that we are just kidding, but are we? As I was truthful with me about me, I began to change. Given to love is being still and knowing He is God...

February 6, 1982

So, what have I learned about marriage and love over these last thirty-three years? I cannot change Wally! I need to take responsibility for me and my actions! I need to forgive seventy times seven, and maybe even every hour if necessary...not for him, but for me, as this influences my love and care for him. My heart filled with unforgiveness only destroys the marriage. My heart willing always to forgive builds my marriage. Do I do this all perfectly? Absolutely not, but what is perfect anyway? Given to love is not always perfect...

So, what does a 52 year old and a 53 year old know about love and marriage? Not sure yet, but let me get back to you in another 33 years as these two determined-and-strong-willed individuals walk out this journey called marriage, with God changing each of us, and being okay that sometimes it is only the strings of the vows holding it together. Our love is growing. We are learning to appreciate each other again, as sometimes the years can cause you to take a person for granted if not careful. Oh, yes, love is in the mix, too...but I think love is in the DNA of our determination, and we keep getting back up again because of 1 Corinthians 13...So, what have we learned about marriage? We get back up again! Given to love is determination and a purposed choice everyday...

CHAPTER 2
But Have Not Love

A while back, we were visiting our son in Florida. We were walking downtown and came across a group of people with red signs, and they were yelling things and being a bit aggressive. As I asked my son about them, he said they were there every Friday and Saturday night and they were from a certain church. They were telling people they were going to hell. They were not nice about it. After we passed them, my non-believing son told me that it is people like that who make him not want anything to do with church or God. I told him I did not blame him. I was embarrassed, and told him that I, also, did not agree with their approach. When we went back to our hotel that night I could not sleep. They upset me because they were coming across as representing the God I love and serve. I prayed for them.

As I was talking to the Lord about it, He reminded me of 1 Corinthians 13:1, "Though I speak with the tongues of men and of angels, but have not love, I have become sounding brass or a clanging cymbal." Wow, they were clanging cymbals. It made me think...can we have the right motives but the wrong approach? What makes the difference? Love makes the difference, but didn't they have love? They were caring about the souls of everyone who walked by, isn't this love? I was learning something very valuable from the experience. I was gaining understanding of love. What were they missing? They were not listening. They were not understanding how they were being received. They were not being heard in the way they would have liked. They were irritating people. I saw and experienced first-hand the sounding brass and the clanging cymbal.

After that, I was much more careful how I spoke and listened to my son, to my husband, and to others with whom I cross paths. I have become a better listener, and I work very hard at not forcing my beliefs on others. I try to put on verses 4-8 in 1 Corinthians 13 and allow it to influence how I sound.

The Apostle Paul does not just write about how we sound or speak, but, also, what we do with our gifts and our giving. Take a look at verses 2-3, "And though I have the gift of prophecy and understand all mysteries and all knowledge, and though I have all faith, so that I could remove mountains, but have not love, I am nothing. And though I bestow all of my goods to feed the poor and though I give my body to be burned, but have not love, it profits me nothing." Love needs to be the driving force behind and within everything.

I have shared my revelations with people when I was younger, and I went to them so excited at my discovery only to hear, "I already know that." I was deflated. Or I was all excited about a book and I would hear the same response. When I heard these words, I felt less than and inferior to them, as I, obviously, was behind. I found it hard to pick up the book. Those little comments we make to others who excitedly come to us can hinder them, (I am guilty of this very thing). What would love look like in these situations? Love would listen and be excited about the discovery, because the discovery is not about the person hearing, but the person sharing. We can allow the enemy to put us up on a pedestal with our gifts, and then we can begin viewing the world around us as less than. The enemy wants us to keep our eyes on ourselves and make everything about us. We are, then, nothing and do not even realize it.

What about giving? Do we value our worth by how much we give? Do we do this? Are we giving to be recognized? Can we do all about which Paul has written and not have love, or worse yet, not recognize our lack of love, and that we actually have nothing? As I was thinking about all of this, I connected it with verse 11 of the same chapter, "When I was a child, I spoke as a child, I understood as a child, I thought as a child; but when I became a man, I put away childish things." This felt totally connected to the first three verses. Without love we are childish...but we have a choice and can mature as we choose to pay attention and allow love to be the driving influence of our words, our actions, our thoughts, our behavior, the way we listen, give, help, care and witness to the world around us.

Paul is writing from experience and understanding. The middle part of this chapter is familiar to many of us, as we hear it at weddings, and people quote it. But overlooking the whole of the chapter we miss something vital. The middle verses are what hold everything else together. It is the meat of the sandwich. Without the meat, we do not have a sandwich, and without the other two sides of the meat, we, also, do not have a sandwich. It is a complete package.

Ask the Lord to hold you accountable to these verses, and to show you when you are not operating out of love. I have been surprised at how many areas the Lord has had me change, because the way I worded something or did something offended someone else and they stopped listening. When I stopped them, relationships changed. I do not have this all figured out, but I am allowing it to be worked out in my daily life of being given to love...

CHAPTER 3
Love Is

There are so many different ways to look at and evaluate 1 Corinthians 13:4-8, I think it will be a lifetime adventure of discovery for me. I have spent many hours reading it, praying into it, and asking the Lord to please give me this love for others. I think, at times, we have a challenge even believing He loves us this way, but He does. Awhile back, I did a verse by verse evaluation of these verses, and so I will share my ponderings...

1 Corinthians 13:4, "Love suffers long and is kind; love does not envy; love does not parade itself, is not puffed up;"

Read that several times...This is what Paul has experienced about the characteristics of the love of God. The same Paul who wrote Romans 8:38-39 and Ephesians 3:14-21. As I read the list, I seemed to encounter it from many views all at the same time. I viewed it from the perspective of, this is what the love of God is for me, and for others around me. This is what my love should be like for others. And then, I thought of what I have encountered in my life under the term 'love', and how my mind has come to a conclusion, or developed a perception, of this word love because of how I have been treated by others who say they love me.

If you watch movies or television, this is not how love is portrayed. Love is portrayed as an emotion, or feeling, or even an act. How many times have we, personally, encountered people who told us they loved us but they actually did the opposite of these words above? Does this mess with our concept or perception of love? Absolutely! So we have this perception in our heads of what we have learned from others and the world around us of love, and then we try to get our heads around what His love is...how do we do this? This is the love Paul is talking about in the first three verses of this chapter... this is the love we are to give to the people in our lives, but how?

It is one thing to say it and know it, but how do we activate this love within us to give? I am finding that it is one day at a time, one situation at a time. I am, daily, submitting to this list and asking the Lord to give me this type of love. For me, it is starting with my family. I want always to have love that suffers long with another person. I want love that is always kind, no matter how I am feeling. I want love that does not envy, ever. I want love that does not parade itself. To me, that seems like pride. I could be wrong, but that is how I am seeing it at the moment. I want love that is not puffed up. To me, this seems like a false love that is focused on self. Do we do the opposite of these and not realize it? These are not emotions, these are attitudes, thoughts, choices, and focus...I encourage you turn this into a prayer for you.

1 Corinthians 13:5, "does not behave rudely, does not seek its own, is not provoked, thinks no evil;"

I look at this list and am encouraged that this is His love toward me. Then, I look at the list as a measuring rod for my love for others and see that I fall short, but I know that it is possible with Him. We constantly encounter these situations with other people. I have had many people behave rudely, seek their own, be provoked and think evil, and when we, personally, encounter these, they have the potential to raise the same thing up in us if we are not mindful of them. I think we do encounter these people to teach us, to train us, and to expose this within us so it can be changed. I, personally, want enough love within me not to behave rudely, not to seek my own, not to be provoked, and to think no evil. For now, it is my prayer, and I am thankful that each day is filled with opportunities to learn. It is interesting that, in the eyes of the world, the opposite of this is how you get ahead in life. The movies and television shows are filled with this and people laugh at it. Can the opposite of this list be learned and picked up as we walk through life? The only way to even begin to walk in these is to have a heart and mind that forgives quickly. Unforgiveness responds with the opposite of each of these...*My prayer is, Help me, Lord Jesus, always to choose these in each situation that comes to test them in me...*

1 Corinthians 13:6, "does not rejoice in iniquity, but rejoices in the truth;"

I wonder how many times we rejoice or laugh at the expense of another person. Maybe we do not laugh at an iniquity (sin), but we do laugh, at times, when someone is in an embarrassing situation or being put down. Then, I do think of people who do actually rejoice in the fact that someone did something wrong. Maybe some have been on the receiving end of this, and it is not fun. I, personally, think when someone is rejoicing in the fall of another person, they were jealous of them, and that is sad.

The second half of this verse is rejoicing in the truth. This, to me, is easy to do when it is good truth, or the truth about a situation comes out and all the false lies get exposed. But does this mean that our love is to rejoice in the truth when the truth about someone has severe consequences because of it? What about when the truth hurts; can we choose to rejoice in it? It makes me wonder if rejoicing in the truth in some situations could be rejoicing in iniquity as the truth exposes it... What is this really saying? Think about it...

1 Corinthians 13:7, "bears all things, believes all things, hopes all things, endures all things."

I am encouraged that this is the love He has for me/us. His love will and can bear all things! Believes all things, is an interesting statement. I want to think this would mean that He believes in me. We all want someone to believe in us, believe that we can do it, believe that we can make it through and be all that we can be. He believes all things for us in our present and future. To me, this is saying He is our biggest fan and is right there with us. He hopes all things for us and endures all things for and with us. He has hope for us and He is able to endure with us, which Paul explains further in Romans 8:38-39, when he writes that nothing can separate us from the love of God.

So, this is His unfailing, steadfast love for us. But how do we line up with this love for others? I want to have this love for my husband and children, and I am pursuing it daily, but, at this point, it is not always my first choice. It is, also, not always my first choice, or response, with other people around me. What would it look like if we had this love for the people in our lives? There is a conflict that arises with the world views on these areas. We want this, but how do we walk this out? For me, this has become my prayer, to have all of the aspects and characteristics of this love in verses 4-8 of this chapter. As I focus on them daily, I begin to recognize when I am given a choice to choose one of them in different situations throughout my day...Help us, Holy Spirit!

1 Corinthians 13:8, "Love never fails."

If we read in Luke 23, about the last moments of Jesus' life, we see His love that never fails. I thought of the times when I have been sick with a very bad cold, and my head was so stuffed up that I could not think, and my body ached so badly I did not want to move. I thought of those moments of sickness where you just close your eyes and want it to be over, where you are exhausted and do not want anyone to ask you a thing. I thought of the many people who I have watched fight with cancer, and the exhausted-give-up moment they come face to face with. Jesus reached that place, but what was different was, He did not give up, He did not quit, He did not complain, He did not wavier from the plan, even though, at any point in time, He had all power and authority to stop it. Wow, that is love that does not fail. I am so amazed at His love that does not fail. Read Luke 23 from the perspective of what He endured and you will see love that never fails. As you read it, think about the times you have been exhausted, or sick, or falsely accused of something, that moment in time when life looks impossible and pain is overwhelming. His love never fails, and He lived it out to show us His love. Encounter His love today in a new and fresh way. Until we receive this unfailing love, we will not be able to give it.

Embrace these verses in 1 Corinthians 13:4-8, study them, pray into them, ask the Holy Spirit to hold you accountable to living them. Look them up in other versions. Write them on a 3 x 5 card and tape them to your mirror to remind yourself of them. There are sixteen of them, purpose to focus on one each day. Every one of these is a choice we can make...Are you given to love? Relationships will be different...but you cannot give what you do not have, so ask for it, fight for it, seek it, desire it, embrace it, and enjoy it!

CHAPTER 4

His Top 10

How do you feel about "The Ten Commandments"? Have you thought about them lately? If it has been awhile, I encourage you to take some time and read the chapters that contain them. You can find them in Exodus chapter 20 and Deuteronomy chapter 5. For purposes of this chapter, I will be referencing out of Exodus 20. *(Warning this will be the longest chapter in this book, take some time with it. Take a slow walk through it with God.)* I always viewed "The Ten Commandments" as a list of rules and regulations God gave to a group of out-of-control-people, and for a time in the past. I did not see them as for me today. I especially did not see them as love, but as a way to control and tell me what I could and could not do. How do you view them? Think about it...

Several months back, I felt led by the Lord to read Exodus chapter 20. I spent the next month reading this one chapter repeatedly. As I was reading it, it was reading me. The only way I can put words to what I was experiencing is that, as I was reading it, He would open my understanding, showing me what He intended for it and how I was walking it out. It was almost as if I would read the first commandment and it would knock on the door of my heart and mind and show me how I was doing. I was shocked at the understanding. The simple little things many of us do in everyday life have the potential to lead us away from Him and His best for us, and we do not even realize it. Prior to my time in this chapter, I spent time in Romans 12:1-2, "I beseech you therefore, brethren, by the mercies of God, that you present your bodies a living sacrifice, holy, acceptable to God, which is your reasonable service. And do not be conformed to this world, but be transformed by the renewing of your mind, that you may prove what is that good and acceptable and perfect will of God."

Romans 12:1-2, became my prayer. Lord, help me to present my body as a living sacrifice, holy, acceptable to You. Help me not to be conformed to this world and the way it thinks, and may the struggles I encounter in this world transform me as I press into You to renew my mind so that I may prove what is that good and acceptable and perfect will of God in my life. I believe this prayer was being answered as I read Exodus 20. He was renewing my mind as I read His Word. (You can make this your prayer too.)

I would like to offer a different perspective of "The Ten Commandments". What if these "Top 10" were viewed from the perspective of love? As I read through them, I thought about God being love (1 John 4:16) and how

He would have given these for our protection. He gave these to help us and to make us aware of all the ways and situations we would encounter that have the potential to, little by little, lead us away from His best for us. He knew the schemes the enemy would set in place. He knew the temptations to be conformed to the world, and to fit in and not make waves. He knew the subtle little ways that one choice at a time could slowly lead us away from God and we would not even be aware of it. I will take you on a little bit of the journey I encountered as I read them each day...

Exodus chapter 20 begins with, "And God spoke all these words". When I hear verses that begin this way, I pay attention. He only speaks what is necessary. He does not speak to just speak. He has a purpose with each word. He is intentional when He speaks. The Creator of everything, all knowing, perfect, complete, lacking in nothing, God of possible, all wise, full of strength and power, faithful, God of complete love, holy God is speaking...are we listening? I was and continue to be. There is a purpose to the order. There is a purpose for each one. Each of these is for our success in life, and to have the most amazing relationship with God the Father, Jesus our Savior, and the Holy Spirit, our Helper. He then speaks, "I am the LORD your God." I stopped at those words and felt their importance. I heard questions rise up within me, "Is He the Lord my God?" My first response is absolutely, and then the journey began as He answered that question with His top 10...

The first one is *"You shall have no other gods before Me."* Period, no explanation, no sugar coating, just you shall have no other gods before Me. I, then, began to live out the next few days of tests and trials that showed me the other gods I did have before Him, and, also, how I had gotten in the way of God in the lives of others I loved. I discovered money was a god before Him as situations arose where we had unexpected expenses and I found myself worrying. I repented. I then discovered that our temporary money shortage was exposing how I really felt. It exposed that when we had our business, I thought I created the success. I felt that in our current situation I could be doing a better job than God in supplying for our needs. I was the god before God. I repented and asked Him to forgive me.

Situations arose where one of my children was going through a challenging time and I was worrying. I found myself trying to protect them. My prayers on their behalf were crying out for mercy. He showed me I was not trusting Him and I felt I knew better than He did what was best for them. Yikes, I was the god before God. I repented and addressed why I was thinking this way. There were times, in the past, where we had fully trusted God and it did not turn out the way we thought it should, and I had not addressed that, and it created in me a place that did not fully trust God to take care of us. I repented and I forgave God. I forgave myself, too. There were many of these little situations left unaddressed from my past that created in me a place where I did not trust God, and so, I felt I knew better than God and became the god. I was not aware of this happening, but as I read His word, it read me and I repented...

I was praying, one morning, over a challenging situation with another person, and as I was praying, the Lord showed me I was trying to tell Him what to do. I stopped.

I thought about what I was saying. He was right. I thought I knew better than God what should or should not happen. I was the god as I was praying. I repented and asked Him how to pray...

The second one is *"You shall not make for yourself a carved image."* He brought to mind people who I have valued too highly. He showed me leaders who I placed on a pedestal and then was disappointed when they made a mistake. I had allowed them to have a louder voice than God in situations. The carved image can be in our mind. The carved image can be a false perception. I saw it as anything that I allow to have a louder voice or stronger influence than God in my life. I repented and asked the Lord to forgive me. I also forgave myself. I had to do a lot of repenting and forgiving, because this is how we position ourselves to be transformed. He was renewing my mind. His word was coming alive inside of me. I was walking in the Book of Psalms as I walked through 'The Ten Commandments', spoken to me by the LORD my God.

The third one is *"You shall not take the name of the LORD your God in vain."* I knew that it meant not to use God's name in anger. I felt I knew what this meant, so I repented of the times when I, most likely, did this, and asked Him for forgiveness, and I forgave myself. He then showed me the times I have been around others who have done this and I said nothing. He showed me movies and televisions shows we watch that use His name in vain and we sit there and listen to it. We can become calloused to the use of His name in vain and soon not even hear it or be offended by it. This is the enemies plan to separate us from the LORD our God, one word at a time. He knew, so He planned, in love, to show us and make us aware of it. Needless to say, I repented and asked Him to forgive me and, yes, I forgave myself.

The fourth one is, *"Remember the Sabbath day, to keep it holy. Six days you shall labor and do all your work, but the seventh day is the Sabbath of the LORD your God."* May I suggest that the focus is on the working for six days and giving the seventh to God? In my head it was Sunday as the day of rest or given to the God. I would go to church and then would do some errands while in town, or do some laundry when I got home, or other tasks such as mow the lawn, or a variety of other things. He was speaking to me about my time management. I had come to a place where Sunday had become my catch up day. I was not giving Him the full day. But even as I am writing this, I think it is about what we do with six days of the week so that the seventh day is fully free to be given to Him. Not the name of the day of the week, but the position of the seventh day coming after six days of working. He created us to spend time with Him. He created us to need rest. He modeled it when He created everything around us. He is not saying do as I say and not as I do, but He did it. It is important to who we are, and a vital necessity to our fulfillment of our purpose here on earth. The enemy continually tries to get us not to see it this way, and God knew he would, so, in His love, He gave us this commandment.

The fifth one is, *"Honor your father and your mother, that your days may be long upon the land which the LORD your God is giving you."* As I read this the first few times, little thoughts would pop into my mind of, "Yes, but what about when they?" "But they do not deserve it, or remember what they did?" I heard these little questions that were lying to me about honor. These little questions were poison to my mind, my heart, my soul, my strength, and my future. They were operating in the background of my mind, rationalizing and justifying why they did not deserve it or had not earned it. Honoring my father and mother was not just meaning the words I spoke, or only applied to if they were alive or not, or even if I knew them or not, it begins in the thoughts I think and the actions I take. Forgiving them was honoring in God's eyes. Blessing them was honoring. Giving to them was honoring. Being thankful for all they did for me, and for being a part of me even taking a breath in this world. It affects my attitude toward God and them. I spent a lot of time repenting and asking Him to forgive me and forgiving myself, and then asking Him to show me how to honor my parents the way He desires and not how the world views honoring.

The sixth one is, *"You shall not murder."* This one seemed like an easy one for me to quickly step over; I have never physically murdered anyone and I have no intention of doing it. To me, it has always been viewed as an obvious thing. Even the world believes this, and people who murder other people get punished when caught. What surprised me was when He showed me my thoughts. I saw how I can allow negative thoughts to destroy relationships. I have full potential within my mind to murder and no one would even know it, but He does. He knows that this destroys relationship on every level from parents to children, children to parents, siblings, friends, people in our church, neighbors, those we drive along side of in traffic; the list is endless and it begins in our minds. Unforgiveness is definitely an open door to this. We understand the obvious, but the hidden part can even be hidden to us. Ask Him about your thoughts; I was surprised about mine...

The seventh one is, *"You shall not commit adultery."* This includes our thought life. I was reminded of how subtle the enemy is on this one with television and movies. If we allow ourselves time to view these things or read about them in novels, it breaks down our awareness of how wrong it truly is. Our thoughts can rationalize and justify just about anything when left on their own unguarded. The enemy wants us to think our thoughts belong to us and they are private and harm no one. If he is allowed to get us to ponder it in our thoughts, eventually he gets us to contemplate walking it out. This one, as with all of them, destroys us from the inside out. So much destruction comes to us and the ones we love, and it separates us from God in the process...

Number eight is, *"You shall not steal."* To me, this seemed obvious, also, until He showed me times when I have purchased an album on iTunes and then burned it on a CD and gave it to someone (I stole from the artist). The times when a charge did not get charged that should have been and I chose to say nothing. Surely this did not mean time. Can we steal time, Lord? What is He really talking about that we are not to steal? Is stealing anything we should have paid for but we did not? Is stealing anything we have taken that we did not have permission to take? Can we steal something in our minds and not actually carry it out and feel this is acceptable as long as it remains in our minds and harms no one? Can we steal an idea of someone else? Oh, my mind was really going crazy as I read these four seemingly innocent words. Bottom line...choosing to do this brings harm to relationships with others and with Him. Again, my mind was getting renewed...

Number nine is, *"You shall not bear false witness against your neighbor."* Oh my, He showed me that this includes gossip and making false accusations. We can even allow a false perception of how we think about another person to occupy our thoughts and then we speak that to others about our neighbor. I heard inside of my head the question of, "Who is my neighbor?" Is our neighbor anyone with whom we cross paths? What if our neighbor is family? What if our neighbor is God? Can our actions bear false witness? Can we speak something about someone else that is inaccurate and be convinced that as long as it harms no one it is acceptable? Unforgiveness definitely sets us up to walk right into this as the door to jealousy or offense opens, and bearing false witness seems justified or even revengeful. Can a simple complaint overheard by another bear a false witness? What about those children sitting in the backseat of the car listening to the conversation between you and your spouse? What about the conversations when you are on your cell phone in a public place? How does television, movies and novels influence this? How does the world view this? I repented as the questions came flooding out when I read this...He began the renewing of my mind, yet again...

Number ten is, *"You shall not covet your neighbor's house; you shall not covet your neighbor's wife, nor his male servant, nor his female servant, nor his ox, nor his donkey, nor anything that is your neighbor's."* Covet means to desire or lust. It is not the wanting of something that is wrong, but wanting it at the expense of others, or from a motive of jealousy or envy (this meaning was taken from the footnotes of my Spirit-filled Life Bible). Some of this list is simple, and in my case, does not even apply, or does it? I understand the house and wife area, but since it does not say husband, does that mean that it is okay? Certainly not! We might also skip over the servant part, but could this be viewed as someone our neighbor hires to work for them, gardener, house cleaner, or other things? The ox and the donkey seem to be easy, but are they? Are they symbolic? What do they represent? But just in case you were looking for a loophole, it is concluded with 'anything' that is your neighbor's. This, again, begins in our thoughts. To me, this summed up all the other nine. I repented, yet again…

All of these, when chosen not to heed, bring harm to our relationships with others and with Him, the LORD our God. They are all given in love to create in us a great ability to love. They are all the ways the enemy tries to break down our love, to destroy relationships, and to get our focus away from our purpose and destiny. Although this chapter is long, I do hope that your perspective of "The Ten Commandments" has changed, and that you now see them through the eyes of love. For God so loved that He gave His Son, and His Son, Jesus, summed up the ten into two in Mark 12:30-31, "'And you shall love the LORD your God with all of your heart, with all of your soul, with all of your mind, and with all of your strength.' This is the first commandment. 'And the second, like it, is this: 'You shall love your neighbor as yourself." There is no other commandment greater than these."

All of the commandments are about love. What influences our love. What changes our love. What enhances our love. How to fully receive and give love. The original ten and the new two are given in love and to love. They are necessary for us to be given to love...

CHAPTER 5
Love Yourself

Do you love or even like yourself? Think about it... Unfortunately, many will say they do not really love or like who they are. When Jesus is asked the question of the first commandment of all by the scribes in Mark 12:28, His response is found in Mark 12:30-31, "'And you shall love the LORD your God with all of your heart, with all of your soul, with all of your mind, and with all of your strength.' This is the first commandment. 'And the second, like it, is this: 'You shall love your neighbor as yourself.'" There is no other commandment greater than these."

The second, like it, is this...You shall love your neighbor as yourself. This communicates that we can only love our neighbor as much as we love ourselves. I think this is very telling if we look around us and see how people are treating people. Getting a little closer to home, how we ourselves treat the people around us shows us how we love ourselves. Why is it so challenging to love ourselves?

We have history with ourselves. We know what we have done, the choices we have made, the thoughts we have thought, the lies we have told, the words, the failures, the unfulfilled dreams we have dreamt, we have also been told by the world that we do not measure up... we live with ourselves day in and day out. We might not like the size of our body, the color of our skin, the gender that we are, the education we have, the job we are at, the money we make, the house that we are in, the relationships we have had, the way we have been treated, and the list goes on for days. All of this history contributes to how we love and like ourselves.

So, how in the world do we sort through all of this history and come to the conclusion of loving ourselves when we have done such a great job of not loving ourselves? For those of you who have read my first book, "Given to Forgive", you know you have to choose to forgive yourself. This can, at times, be very difficult to do, because we know what we have done, we know the pain we have caused, we believe we know the truth about our past, and we convince ourselves that we do not deserve to forgive ourselves. When we choose this, we are on a path of self-destruction, feeling we deserve to be punished, and whether we are fully aware of it or not, it is happening until we forgive ourselves. Stop for a moment...Do you need to forgive yourself? Remember that God forgives you when you ask, and He feels you deserve to be forgiven...maybe it is time to come into agreement with forgiving yourself.

LOVE YOURSELF

I, personally, have had to do a lot of forgiving of myself. I had to remove the whether I deserve it or not, out of the processing. I had to make the choice to begin forgiving myself of the choices I have made that did not work out the way I thought they should have and went into the 'failure' column of my life history. I had to choose to trust that if He could forgive me, I could forgive me. I started with the big ones first that the Holy Spirit brought to my mind. I asked the Lord to forgive me for what I did, and also, for holding onto it and not forgiving myself. I had to ask Him to forgive me for thinking I know what I deserved better than He knows. I, then, forgave myself for each item. This was not a one-time-sit-down with the Lord, but many. I had a big list. I did not love or like myself. I was holding many things against myself. I realized that if I could not love or like myself, I certainly could not love or like anyone else anymore than I thought of myself. I also could not love or like God anymore than I loved or liked myself. So, I forgave myself and continue to forgive myself to this day. I have worked through much of my past, but I do purpose to keep a short account with myself and include it in every situation where I am forgiving another person...I forgive myself. It does get easier as you experience the freedom of forgiveness.

I, also, realized I needed to purpose to be thankful for who I was and who I am. One day, I began thanking the Lord for who He made me to be. I got very specific. I thanked Him for the color and texture of my hair, for my head, my mind, my ears, my eyes and the color of my eyes, my nose, my mouth, the sound of my voice, my tongue and my ability to taste, my teeth, my cheek bones, my bone structure, my blood, my veins, my organs (in as much detail as I could think of), my tendons, ligaments, joints, muscles, arms, legs, fingers, and toes. I sat there and thanked Him for creating me a female. I was speaking life into my body. I could feel it. My perspective of me was changing. I began taking better care of my body and made better choices with the foods I ate, and the exercise I did. I found a new desire to care about what I watched, listened to, and thought. I found motivation to care for and value me.

I realized I was not going to be able to love the LORD my God with all of my heart, soul, mind, and strength unless I loved and cared for myself first. Many times I thanked Him for who He made me to be. I wanted all of me to come into agreement with being thankful, that I was not a mistake, and no matter who the world said or thought I was, I was created by God and He does not make mistakes. He loves me. He has a plan for who I am, and everything about me has a purpose to work together for good. He chose everything about me. I am fearfully and wonderfully made. I found myself liking and loving myself as I forgave and was thankful. If I chose the worlds way of thinking, I would not forgive myself, because I did not deserve it, and I would not measure up to the magazines and pictures that tempt us to compare. My mind was being renewed through forgiveness and thankfulness.

The more I loved myself, the more I was able to love others. We cannot give what we do not have. I would encourage you to forgive yourself, let yourself off the hook, it is time. I would also encourage you to take some time each day to thank Him for every part of your physical body. I do believe that healing on many levels will take place and transformation will begin...the best part about all of this...you can do this anywhere. We can forgive ourselves and thank Him as we wait in traffic, sitting in the dentist chair, while in the shower, while waiting in a line, when it is dark or light out, anytime and anywhere...He made me in love to love...

Romans 12:1-2 at work...

CHAPTER 6
Heart to Heart

I love the Psalms. I always feel like I am reading someone's journal as they process the struggles of life and pain and they look for God in them. Many of them begin with their struggle of calling out to what must have felt like a distant God, and conclude with Him coming close, and their response to it. If we draw near to God, He will draw near to us (James 4:8). He will come as close as we allow Him to come. The writers of Psalms always knew where to go, and we get to read about the moments as they find Him. We can learn so much from them. They are real. Did they write thinking someone was going to read their private thoughts thousands of years later? No. I have favorites, and the ones I feel I have fully embraced and have submitted to, I draw a little flag in my Bible and write the word 'MINE' on the flag. I claim it as mine. I give the Lord full permission to work it deep into me. I do not ever want Him to stop teaching me and pulling my life through those very chapters. One such chapter is Psalm 139. David, the man after God's own heart, wrote it. The title over this chapter in my Bible reads, 'God's Perfect Knowledge of Man'.

I have spent countless hours digging into this Psalm wanting to discover what David did when he wrote it. We have the opportunity to connect with their revelation, just as you can connect with mine. So, let me take you on a journey of discovery into Psalm 139... (If you have not read it in awhile, stop and read it before continuing... take your time).

I have viewed this chapter from many angles. One of the perspectives is to view it from God's perspective in verses 1-18. If God Himself were to write this to you, this is what it would say...

*O My Child, I have searched for you and known you.
I know your sitting down and your rising up; I understand your thought afar off.
I comprehend your path and your lying down, and I'm acquainted with all your ways.
For there is not a word on your tongue, but behold, O Child, I know it altogether.
I have hedged you behind and before, and laid My hand upon you.
Such knowledge is too wonderful for you; it is high, you cannot attain it.
Where can you go from My Spirit?
Or where can you flee from My Presence?
If you ascend into heaven, I am there;
If you make your bed in hell, behold, I am there.
If you take the wings of the morning, and dwell in the uttermost parts of the sea, even there My hand shall lead you, and My right hand shall hold you.*

If you say, "Surely the darkness shall fall on me,"
Even the night shall be light about me;
Indeed, the darkness shall not hide from Me,
but the night shines as the day; the darkness and the light are both alike to Me.
For I formed your inward parts;
I covered you in your mother's womb.
You will praise Me, for you are fearfully and wonderfully made; Marvelous are My works,
and that your soul knows very well.
Your frame was not hidden from Me,
when I made you in secret, and skillfully wrought in the lowest parts of the earth.
My eyes saw your substance, being yet unformed.
And in My book they were written, the days fashioned for you, when as yet there were none of them.
How precious also are My thoughts to you,
O My Child! How great is the sum of them!
If I should count them, they would be more in number than the sand; When you awake, I am still with you.

Do you see His love for you? Do you see His care to every detail of your life? He is involved in your life...He loves you. He is committed to loving you. He is given to love you!

Now, let's step into this listening to David. Let's listen as David's heart after God connects with God's heart after his...

I hear the first two verses as David becoming aware of God... *listen...*

> *O LORD, You have searched me and known me.*

*You know my sitting down and my rising up;
You understand my thought afar off.*

Then in verses 3-12, I hear David connecting to the love God has for him, the faithfulness of God to him, and the assurance and security he has with God and in God... *listen...*

*You comprehend my path and my lying down, and are
acquainted with all my ways.
For there is not a word on my tongue, but behold,
O LORD, You know it altogether.
You have hedged me behind and before,
and laid Your hand upon me.
Such knowledge is too wonderful for me;
It is high, I cannot attain it.
Where can I go from Your Spirit? Or where
can I flee from Your presence?
If I ascend into heaven, You are there;
If I make my bed in hell, behold, You are there.
If I take the wings of the morning,
and dwell in the uttermost parts of the sea,
Even there Your hand shall lead me,
and Your right hand shall hold me.
If I say, "Surely the darkness shall fall on me,"
even the night shall be light about me;
Indeed, the darkness shall not hide from You,
but the night shines as the day;
The darkness and the light are both alike to You.*

In verses 13-16, I hear David connecting to his purpose and feeling like he belongs. He discovers as he gets into God's heart for him, that he is not an accident and that God was involved and intentional about his existence the second it began... *listen...*

*For You formed my inward parts; You covered me
in my mother's womb.
I will praise You, for I am fearfully
and wonderfully made;
Marvelous are Your works, and that my soul
knows very well.
My frame was not hidden from You,
when I was made in secret,
And skillfully wrought in the lowest parts of the earth.
Your eyes saw my substance, being yet unformed.
And in Your book they all were written,
the days fashioned for me,
When as yet there were none of them.*

In verses 17-18, I hear their hearts coming together and David is inside of the love of God for him in its purist form... *listen...*

*How precious also are Your thoughts to me, O God!
How great is the sum of them!
If I should count them, they would be more
in number than the sand;
When I awake, I am still with You.*

In verses 19-22, we hear David's courage awakening... the courage we heard him say to the Philistine in 1 Samuel 17. He is seeing the world around him from God's perspective, not his own. It is as if he is now sitting right next to God talking... *listen...*

*Oh, that You would slay the wicked, O God!
Depart from me, therefore, you bloodthirsty men.
For they speak against You wickedly;
Your enemies take Your name in vain.
Do I not hate them, O LORD, who hate You?*

> *And do I not loathe those who rise up against You?*
> *I hate them with perfect hatred;*
> *I count them my enemies.*

The final two verses, 23-24, are where David fully trusts and surrenders to God in every way possible... *listen...*

> *Search me, O God, and know my heart;*
> *Try me, and know my anxieties;*
> *And see if there is any wicked way in me,*
> *and lead me in the way everlasting.*

Can you see the potential that is available to you? Oh, this Psalm is such a gift to us. I have asked God to search me and know my heart...It is interesting that God does know my heart, I just do not always know it. I have come to a point in my life where God is the only One I fully and completely trust with these final two verses. He is not going to give me advice that is wrong. He knows everything about me and how I think. He knows what I have been through, heard, experienced and how I process things. He knows what I do not know and knows just how to get me to know it. He will not stop answering this prayer of mine until it is fully answered. I love how thorough He is when answering. I have history with Him now and I trust Him with the secret things of my heart. The things I tell no one else. He does not yell at me. He always tells me the truth. He loves me completely and I trust His love for me. He is committed to loving me completely forever. He is always for me. Do you trust Him at this level? He loves you completely and purely. He made you in love, with love, and to love. I pray that you will discover this at a deeper level for you...

CHAPTER 7
Are You Persuaded?

How do we learn about love? When we are young, and as we grow up, we learn love from our parents, our family, our friends, relationships, and the world that is around us. If any of these are broken, angry, hurting, and making choices that bring destruction, then our view and understanding of love gets influenced by this. Our environment teaches us about love, good and bad. It was no different for me. I came from a broken home with an alcoholic parent. There was fighting, anger, hurt, discouragement, failure, and no Jesus. My view of love was distorted. I have been lied to, and had many broken promises. My understanding of love was, you cannot trust it. I did not start out being given to love. I did not understand love. I had to learn it as I walked out life with Jesus, starting back when I was 17 years old. I am now 53, almost 54 years old, you do the math. This was not an overnight revelation. I do not think that I was given to love until about 13 years ago...

Paul learned about God's love, too...through life experiences with God. He wrote much of the New Testament, but he did not start out being given to love. He was driven to destroy Christians until he encountered Jesus. He was then given to love. This is what he learned about how given God is to love...Romans 8:38-39, "For I am persuaded (convinced) that neither death nor life, nor angels nor principalities nor powers, nor things present nor things to come, nor height nor depth, nor any other created thing (includes people), shall be able to separate us from the love of God, which is in Christ Jesus our Lord." The bracketed words are my addition.

In my Bible, I have written that Cheryl is persuaded...I, too, have learned. What Paul has written is God's side of being given to love us! Think about it. As He is given to love us, He has an expectation for us to love others through Christ Jesus. He does not expect us to figure it all out overnight. He knows that it is learned. He knows that it is experience. That is why He is given to love us through all, because He knows it takes all to learn how to be given to love. Think about what all of the men and women in the Bible went through as they were learning. They are there to show us it is possible, and also, that there are times when we mess up, but when we mess up and discover God still loves us, we become more given to love back.

We have an enemy, in case you were not aware of it. He uses the world around us to break our love and trust in God. He uses anyone who is willing to be used, as in my case. But as I read His word, forgive, and spend time with Jesus...I discovered His love for me and that changes me.

ARE YOU PERSUADED?

Are you convinced that nothing can separate you from the love of God? If not, ask Him to show you why? What got set up? So many times we view God from the view of our life experiences and how people have treated us. We encounter many people who distort that view and how He sees us.

Maybe you grew up with wonderful examples of love, praise God, but there are many around you who did not. Help them...be given to love them, the ones who hate you, gossip about you, lie to you, steal from you, disappoint you, mislead you, spitefully use you, and do not know how to love...those, the lost, the ones in need, the angry, yes, the ones who smell, and are even homeless. Be given to love the ones no one chooses to love, He is...

We learn how to be given to love by loving those who do not love us. We can find God in our struggles with other people. We can find God in those challenging moments. Our daily challenges with the world around us are filled with potential to learn about the love of God for us. I believe that until we are persuaded that nothing can separate us from the love of God, we cannot believe it for others...We cannot be given to love until we believe that He is given to love us...

CHAPTER 8
For God So Loved

"For God so loved the world that He gave His only begotten Son, that whoever believes in Him should not perish but have everlasting life" (John 3:16). I have spent a lot of time on this Scripture in the past, and yet, I have learned that to pass by the familiar is a foolish choice, as there are always new depths He wants to reveal to us when we stop and look again. In my time of prayer, I became in awe of this Scripture, and as I pressed into it, I found myself repenting for not loving people as He loved.

I pressed into thinking about the Creator of everything, and us in particular, giving us a gift He knew would be rejected, spit on, misunderstood, plotted against, mocked, killed, and, for thousands of years after, the same thing over and over again, but it did not stop Him from giving His only begotten Son out of His love. I repented for the many times I have rejected others because of my perception of their reception of me doing something good for them. Have you done that? Have you chosen not to give a gift to someone because they would not appreciate it? Have you withheld further gifts because you did not receive a thank you from the gifts of the past? I am sorry, but I was repenting, as I saw so clearly my flesh, and pride getting in the way of the love of Jesus that is inside of me wanting to be released.

What is, possibly, rising up in you right now? For me, I saw the times when someone wronged me and so I withheld, but God so loved the world that He gave. For me, I saw how, at times, I did not want to forgive because they did not deserve to be forgiven, but God so loved the world that He gave. I see a world that has for thousands of years chosen to serve other gods, but God so loved the world that He gave. Whatever you have experienced, walked through, heard, received or not received, please allow your flesh to step aside for a moment and focus on the truth that God so loved the world that He gave. He gave His Son for you and me and for all the people around you that you encountered in your yesterdays, in your today, and in your future. The choices and words and responses or reactions of the people around you did not stop Him from loving so much to give His only begotten Son. To me, this Scripture is a reality check and perspective shift.

Jesus was given in love to love. We know that Jesus came as an example (1 Peter 2:21-25). He came to love. Take some time to allow your mind to remember the times Jesus modeled love...What does love look like? Jesus healed, multiplied food, delivered, opened blind eyes, cleansed the leper, raised the dead, and the lame walked, just to write a few. What does love sound like? He spoke truth, He did not have to prove anything, although He could have, and sometimes He did not say a word. Think about 1 Corinthians 13:4-8 and the life of Jesus...interchange the name of Jesus in place of the word love, and we will see He was given to love through all. He had opposition. He had people talking behind His back. He had people who hated Him. He had people who misunderstood Him. He had people who wanted Him to be something He was not. Through everything Jesus walked through, experienced, and did...was love. He was given in love to love and show it to us that we, also, be given in love to love. Everything that He taught, He walked. Whatever excuses want to rise up within our minds of why we do not have to love, He abolished with His example. When we accepted Jesus as our Savior, and the Holy Spirit moved inside of us, we, too, became given to love. It became possible...we cannot do this in our own strength. We need Him. I need Him to be able to be given to love. By choosing Him, I am choosing love...this makes me given! How about you? Try putting your name in the place of the word love...

CHAPTER 9
Given to Love

I have a very good friend who is my hero. I have journeyed through life with her for many years. When I think of being given to love, her and her family's faces are the first ones I think of. Many years ago, she married an amazing man who had a crippling illness. He was in a wheelchair when they married. That did not matter to either of them. They were given to love...

As his illness progressed, his mobility lessened, but it did not stop him from working, loving her, and it did not stop her from loving him. They soon had triplet girls, I had the privilege of praying for each soon after their birth. They were the size of my hand. When they were born, her husband became very ill and was in the hospital. For many months, the girls did not get to come home. I remember sitting on the curb outside of the hospital with her, encouraging her that this would pass and that they were all going to be okay. It did not happen immediately, but they did all come home. The babies and her husband required round the clock care. She did it. She kept on going. She loved beyond what I thought was even humanly possible. She did not complain.

Her husband kept working as the girls grew. She continued to care for all of them. As the girls have grown, her husband's illness has gotten worse. He cannot leave the house. Since he is able to work from home, he continues to work with only the slight movement available in his hand. She has to give him breathing treatments and feed him but she keeps doing it. She does not complain. I see the love in her eyes for him and the love in his eyes for her. Their eyes are their back and forth communication. They simply amaze me at their love for each other. They are given to love for life...

The girls are now in middle school. They are amazing as well. They do not argue. They do not fight. They do not get jealous of each other. If I had not witnessed it year after year, I would not believe how peaceful each of them is. They play well with each other. They help care for their dad, and do not ever complain. They are the most well behaved children I have ever seen. They are given to love because they have received love and experienced it and live it.

All five of them in that house do what needs to be done. This is what family does. The dad does not complain and does not give up. He provides for his family under quite challenging circumstances. He is given to love his wife and girls. He sits in the room where they are playing, watches them, and enjoys everything about them. He is so proud. He is not bitter about his circumstances; he just keeps 'working the plan' as he would say. He is given to love through his attitude and approach toward life.

I love them all so deeply. They are my heroes. They have proved to me that being given to love is not just when everything is going perfect, but it really shines when you have every excuse and reason to complain but you do not. It really shines when you choose to love when you are tired, sick, disabled, and continually have to care for and be cared for day in and day out. They did not have perfect childhoods. They do not have millions of dollars. They do not have a mansion. But they have amazing love. They are given to love through thick and thin, for richer or for poorer, in sickness and in health, until death do they part...and they have given that to the next generation...

CHAPTER 10
Truth in Love

A few months back, I found myself in a situation where I had finally had enough. It was a situation I tolerated in a friendship for several years, and every time we met, I walked away frustrated and felt unheard and misunderstood. They continually gave me advice from their own experience, but did not take the time to listen to my experience, and so, their advice was not accurate. I did not say anything because I did not want to offend or make waves, or open myself up to even more inaccurate advice. I just kept taking it and saying nothing. The time in between visits got greater and greater, as I was avoiding them. Our last visit was all that I was able to take, and I left saying I could not do this anymore...

I had a choice. I could just walk away and never return their calls, emails, or text messages, and eventually they would get the hint, or I could get up the courage and let them know. I knew that it needed to be done in love, not in anger or frustration, so I waited and spent time in prayer until my heart and mind did not want to accuse or blame. Since I am a writer, I chose to write a letter. I like this choice because I can put a lot of thought and prayer into it and read it several times to make sure it is communicating how I feel. A letter also gives them the opportunity to pray and think it through. An unexpected phone call or face to face confrontation seems to always catch me unprepared, and I usually walk away thinking I should have said this or that. So, I chose to write. I should have done this several years prior, but I did not. When I felt the letter was ready to send, I sent it.

After I sent it I prayed. I knew it might be a surprise and it could potentially hurt, but walking away without saying anything seemed worse, and it was cowardly. The situation had no opportunity to change by saying nothing, and even if our friendship ended, they knew why, and had an opportunity to see if there was any truth in it to possibly change. What they did with it was their choice. I continued to forgive them as I waited. I had to fight through my fears each day as I waited for a reply. I did assume I would get a response at some point; just the waiting was not enjoyable. I had to take my thoughts captive many times during the day. I sat with the Lord for many hours so that my heart was prepared for any response.

Several weeks passed before I got a short text. In it they said they just got the email and they were sorry, and sorry I felt the way I did. That was it. They removed me as a friend on Facebook and I have never heard from them again. I was sad about the choice that was made.

I had hoped it would go a different way, but although it ended, they are not wondering why, and I am not left with the unspoken challenges I was having. I spoke the truth in love (and courage).

I wish I could say the lesson was learned and over with, but it was not. I think we are continually faced with situations we do not agree with, and so many times we choose to say nothing, and it leaves an unsettled place within us. I know there are people who have walked away from me and have said nothing. I find myself, every once in awhile, wondering what happened.

I have encountered this in group settings where a person was challenging the group with what they were saying, and no one said anything. This happens in families, in churches, with siblings, in marriages, and in the work place. I found myself wanting to walk away and not cause waves. But to walk away and say nothing solves nothing. It only avoids the problem. Guess what? If we are supposed to be learning something, then we will keep encountering it over and over again until we learn it.

So, I spoke the truth in love. I wrote how I felt, very important not to point fingers, as then people get defensive. If we do not speak the truth in love, the situation has no potential to change. We will remain frustrated and upset, and they remain clueless as to a problem. Yes, they have a choice to address the issue, but then it is their choice, for we have done our part. We, also, have to face our fears, as we are the ones who could be the problem, which is why we, at times, find it much easier to say nothing.

So, what do we do with the letters and words that come to us that are not in love? What do we do when we are on the receiving end of such a letter? The first thing I do is pray. I forgive the person if it came harshly. I forgive the person if it came nicely. I ask the Lord to forgive them and me, and I forgive myself. And then, I ask the Lord to show me my part in it, and if there is any truth in it for me to learn. Is this easy? Absolutely not! Is it necessary? I believe it is. I have an opportunity to gain understanding about how I say things or am received. Sometimes it takes me a few days to respond, and if the person is impatient, they just have to wait anyway, because I cannot respond out of my emotions. It is interesting that they may have been thinking about it for a long time, and out of final frustration, write or speak, and they blast me. It can come as a total surprise to me, but they can, at times, lose sight of that and demand a response. I have to resist their pressure. I refuse to blast back. Do I want to? Sometimes, but I do not because it accomplishes nothing and makes it all worse. I know that both of us have something to learn. So I sit with the Lord and process it with Him. Processing situations with other people can be dangerous, as they can, potentially, pick up your offense, and then, not speak wisdom back to you. Be careful...

When I feel I am past the anger or shock, and have processed it through with the Lord, I will then write. I apologize. I recognize their hurt, and I thank them for having the courage to say something. I take responsibility for my part and do not try to tell them how to handle their part. Sometimes I might write a story or situation of when I felt as they did and what I did, but that is as far as I feel I am to go. It takes much self-control. Do I do this perfectly? No. I am learning and I am better than I was years ago. Does it always work out great? No. We speak the truth in love and let the love part drive the situation. Sometimes it is a simple misunderstanding and it gets cleared up quickly. Other times it is not, and maybe I remind them of someone from their past, and I have stirred up past issues. Each situation is different, but I try to have my response be the same. I am given to love first over being right first...

I have a pretty good idea that I am not the only one who has encountered situations like these...I could write a book filled with stories and situations of my personal challenges with this issue, but the response the Lord always has me do is to speak or write the truth in love, and purpose to listen and take responsibility for my part. It takes great courage, and the easy way out is to do nothing, but then, nothing changes for either of us. Both sides have something to learn. Courage opens the door to the potential of greater understanding and change... it does not always work out wonderfully, but I am taking responsibility for my side of the situation with the Lord. I hope that wherever you are in the mix of all of this, you, too, will choose to give truth in love and receive truth in love...it is a choice...

John 8:32..."And you shall know the truth, and the truth shall make you free."

CHAPTER 11
Let Them Be

Over the last few years, I have been made aware of something that happens in the church, not just from observation, but from experience. As I have traveled and spoke at different events and churches, I brought my daughter with me to help with the book table and other needs that arise. It never fails that we have much to talk about on the journey home as she tells me of what people say to her. I am usually listening with my mouth open. I wish they had said those things to me and not my daughter. I am always left with why... sometimes the words are harmful and judgmental... why? This writing might feel like finger pointing, but, I say, if the shoe fits, own it, and then change it...

This has made me look at my own thoughts on pastor's kids and the children of those in leadership of churches. I have, personally, repented of the higher standards and expectations that I have had on them. Why do we feel it is our right to place a standard on them? I wonder if most of our children could live up to the standards that we place on them. Keep reading...

I would like to provide a different perspective. Have we ever considered that those very children have to share their parent or parents with hundreds of other people? How would your children respond to that? Have we ever considered that those in leadership actually have less time than we do to pour into their children? People expect my daughter to have forgiveness all figured out because I wrote a book on it. I do not even have it all figured out. It is a journey that is learned one situation at a time. She actually gets opportunities to get better at it because of the things that are said to her. I do not believe those speaking to her realize how it comes across, but we need to all be more careful with how we come across to others, especially the children of those in leadership.

I understand why many children of pastors hate the church, as they grow up in the church with all of the double standards and unrealistic expectations that get placed on them. How would our own children withstand such an environment? It seems to me, we should all be kinder and even more loving to them. It seems to me, we should all be helping them even more, because we have taken moments away from them with their parents. They are watching how their parents are treated. They are hearing the words of criticism about things in the church. They are hearing what is being spoken. They are feeling the judgment. They are feeling the unrealistic expectations. Yes, they, at times, rebel, but can you blame them?

Can we all agree to change this? Can we all agree to let God set the standard of where they should or should not be in their walk with Him? Can we all agree that we might have unrealistic expectations of their behavior? Can we give the leaders of the church the freedom to allow their children to be children and not continually feel and experience the judgment that rises up when they make what we perceive to be a poor choice? Can we give the grace to them that we want them to give to us? Can we be mindful that these children are sharing their parents with us? They didn't make the choice to be under such a microscope, or given the choice to share or not. Can we pray more and speak less? Can we love more than criticize? Can we give more than we take?

I, on purpose, allow my children to be who they are regardless of what other people think. I want transparency because then it opens the door to transparency. My family, just as leader's families, has to find their own walk with and faith in God. Yes, they have some advantage in that they have access to our time more than others. I just wonder if some of the judgment and criticism comes from jealousy and envy. I do not know what it is, but can we all take responsibility for our behavior. Please do not take from this that something serious happened at one of the places where I recently spoke, but it happens enough that the Lord has opened my eyes to a problem in the church. So, I say again, if the shoe fits, own it, and change it. This could make all the difference to the health of your church...love your leaders through their children by allowing them to be who they are and not who you think they should or should not be... given to love...

CHAPTER 12
Rylee Hope

This is a very special chapter. You will definitely want to get your tissues. I was the counselor in this letter. I got the honor and privilege to meet and be a part of God showing up and bringing healing and understanding to a heart-breaking moment in a young mom's life. Rylee was given to love. Her love will now be given through her mom to love others. This is real life. This happens. There are times that, when we are given to love, we sit with someone who has lost their love. We allow our love to be enough to help them discover theirs again. I asked Janessa if she would write a letter to be included in this book. I have dedicated this book to Rylee Hope. She fulfilled her purpose, and knows Jesus better than anyone reading this book. She is not sad. She is not alone. She is not in pain. It has been an amazing journey of being given to love...

*To my Daughter,
Rylee Hope*

All you ever knew was love. When all I can do is cry because I miss you so, this truth has been a sweet solace to me. I'll never forget the day I found out about you. In some ways, I wish things were different. I wish you had parents who were married and were planning for a baby. But even so, I loved you from the very start and wanted you more than I had ever wanted anything in my entire life. Your daddy and I tried our best to put our differences aside for your sake, and for all the time you were here with us, I think we succeeded.

As my belly began to grow, I talked to you every day. I wanted you to know my voice, and to know you were loved. I never did too much wondering about whether you were a boy or a girl; I somehow just knew you were a girl. I loved being pregnant with you. My tummy was upset most of the time, and I never slept well, but that only mattered so much. After all, I had you as a daughter now, and I could take you with me everywhere I went. I felt so special carrying you, almost like I was the first woman to ever be pregnant. I know that sounds silly, but I guess I just felt so important being your mommy.

About halfway through your life here, I began to get anxious about feeling you kick. When you finally did, it was absolutely magical. My hands were always on my belly. That was the closest I ever came to holding you when your heart was still beating.

I don't remember anything out of the ordinary in my last week with you. I was impatient to meet you. There was work to be done in the nursery, and I could still feel you move. I went to my thirty second week doctor's appointment and heard your beautiful heart beat for the last time. The doctor said everything looked great.

You went to heaven sometime the next day. I wish I knew the exact moment. After all, wouldn't a mother know? As I was getting dinner ready, it dawned on me that I hadn't felt you move all day. I was in shock that I didn't notice it sooner. The short drive to the Emergency Room was the longest I had ever experienced. Every other minute or so, your daddy would ask me if I could feel you, and with tears welling up in my eyes each time, I said, "No." Three nurses, a doctor, and two sonograms later, we were told your precious little heart had stopped beating. I didn't want to believe it, I didn't think I could. Your daddy and I looked at each other in complete shock, and full of pain, we cried. Just moments later, I was told labor would be induced, and I would have to give birth to you, my sweet baby that was already with Jesus. My precious daughter, know that my labor pains were a delight compared to the pain in my heart. With every contraction, came a reminder of what wasn't any more, I cried. With every sound of the laboring women down the hall, I cried. With every newborn cry I heard, I cried. My labor with you lasted about a day and a half. I only pushed for about five minutes and out you came. It was silent. That sound of silence is something I can still hear today. It was as if the whole world was silent.

They put you in my arms, and could only say, "I'm so sorry". You were the most beautiful thing I had ever seen. You were absolutely perfect in every way. I never imagined our meeting would be like that. I wanted to look into your eyes and know you were looking back at me. No, this wasn't the way it was supposed to be. Your daddy and I held you close. We said a prayer together, acknowledging that you were in heaven now, and asking God to give us strength, and one day, beauty for ashes.

Our families came by to meet you. There were so many tears. There were no words, just tears. A precious friend stopped by to take pictures of you. She captured you so beautifully. I'll never get to look at pictures of your first birthday or your wedding day, so I treasure your few pictures with all my heart; I love to look at you.

We spent several hours with you, and with each hour passing I knew we would soon have to say good-bye. I placed you on my bed to wrap you in your blanket one last time. Your precious body was limp and lifeless, my sweet baby, you were so cold. I covered you in tears and kisses. I remember looking at the three of us in a mirror; we made such a beautiful family. Your daddy held you close one last time, and I kissed your forehead. He handed you to the nurse and we said good-bye.

As we left the hospital, we were walking to our car and there was a new mother walking with her baby, too. Her family was videotaping this precious moment. I cried and cried. We walked into our home with empty hands, what seemed like nothing to show for my being pregnant more than eight months and a thirty-hour labor. My milk came in a few days later. It felt like a cruel joke; my own body didn't even know that you had died. There was nothing to do but wait for the milk to dry up, my milk that was supposed to sustain you and help you grow.

We received beautiful flowers and cards, not the kind one receives to be congratulated on a healthy baby, but instead, ones of remorse and sympathy because you, my little one, were not like the rest.

We decided to have your ashes put in a beautiful little heart. We had your name engraved on it. And although you were too much for one heart, because of an accidental mix-up in the ordering, we ended up with two hearts. There was one for your daddy and one for me, which we would each take with us when we went our separate ways a few months later.

In the time that followed your leaving us, I spent all my days missing you. I was depressed and angry. I didn't understand where our God was in all of this. I decided to keep my distance from Him, most of the time avoiding Him altogether. Instead, I would sit in my rocking chair, in the chair I was supposed to rock you in, and tell you how much I missed you, how much I wanted you there. Most days my arms would literally ache to hold you; I felt it was a mother's right. I looked around at all your unfinished quilts and knitted blankets, wondering what I was supposed to do with them.

I happily avoided public places, including church; I let my bible continue to collect dust. My depression worsened. Most days, I didn't want to live anymore. I was mad at God for not giving me the opportunity to give my life for you. I would have gladly taken your place. Of course, now, my darling, I realize how selfish that is. How could I, your mother, ever want to take you away from the perfect love and complete absence of pain you experience in heaven? How could I want to take you away from Jesus?

Then, somehow, by God's grace, I decided to get counseling once a week. Before going, I was angry and felt cheated, but then my heart began to soften. I began to realize that I put all of my hopes and purposes on you. I'm so sorry, Sweetheart, for the burden I made you bear. I placed so much of my future on you, that when you died, I felt like I had died, too. I began to realize that I didn't want you to leave me because I thought I could love you better than your heavenly Papa ever could.

The moment I let go of that lie and asked forgiveness from our Papa, my heart started to heal. I had to come to grips with the fact that He didn't take you away from me, because you were never really mine to begin with; we all belong to God and no one else. With that realization, I knew I would have to let you go. Even though you were already God's, I, personally, had to release you to Him for my heart's sake. Please know Rylee, that it was the hardest thing I have ever had to do.

I realize now it was an act of mercy on God's part in taking you to heaven. You never knew pain and never will. You never had to endure a broken heart, never had to feel rejected, never had to grow up in a broken home, and never had the opportunity to walk away from God. He made the best decision possible for you, and I rejoice in that, because a mother puts the needs of her children before her own. Most people never get to know why things like this happen on this side of heaven. And yet, Papa has graciously shared with me what your purpose was and how He will use this tragedy for good. You were created to change generations, to do a mighty work of love in so many. You were created to save your parents and your future siblings. You have done such great work for His kingdom, and will continue to do so as your legacy lives on.

Often I am so amazed at all that you accomplished in just thirty two short weeks! You have accomplished more than most people do in a full lifetime. It's because of you, that I understand our Papa's love for His children. It's because of you, that I am full to the brim and over flowing with mama love. It's because of you, that I don't want to give up, but instead, press on until I fulfill my purpose.

You make me brave. After all. that is what your name means, "brave hope". I know that when I birthed you, I birthed love as well. And for so long I have been confused as to what to do with this love. I have accepted the fact that you do not need my love. Even though I will love you with all that I am for all of eternity; you are wholly, dearly, and perfectly loved by our Papa in heaven. You lack nothing in Him; you don't need any supplemental love from me.

But finally, little one, I know what to do with all this mama love. Our Papa has called me to be a missionary in Mexico. He has called me to be a mother to the motherless orphans. There are few things that I know I can do well, and at the top of the list is loving like only a mama can with the heart Papa graciously gave me. Our Papa will love through me, and children will know that they are never forgotten, but instead, dearly loved and have a hope and a future. You and our Papa are making all this possible.

I hope I can be a mommy that you can be proud of. I don't want to waste what you have given me; I want to pass it on. I want to be given to love. And please, know that no matter how many other children I mother, both my own and my adopted, you will always be my first. I can never love another exactly like I have loved you, because there will never be another like you. I still cry because I miss you, grief truly is for the living. I'll always have a part of my heart missing until I get to heaven. But I'm so glad to know that I don't ever have to say good-bye for good, our meeting and being together is merely postponed until my job here is finished. Give Papa a big hug and kiss for me. I love you with all of my heart, my sweet baby girl. Your daddy sends all his love.

See you soon!

*Love Mommy,
Janessa Faith*

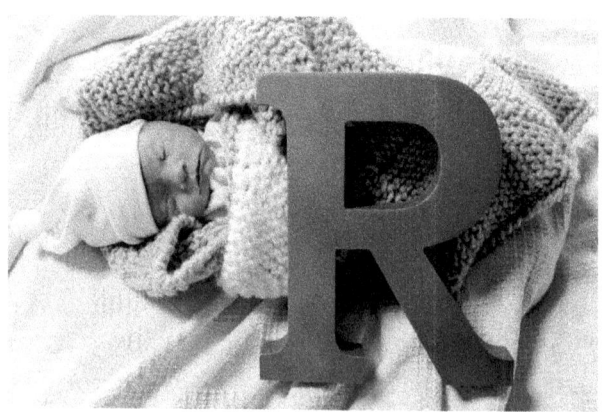

October 25, 2014

CHAPTER 13
Say "Thank-You!"

A while back, my 20 year old son was home for a month for Christmas break. I love having him home. We spent a lot of time together. His girlfriend came out for a visit for part of the time. She had never been to California, so I cleared my schedule and planned places to see. We visited many places from Yosemite to San Francisco and Mt. Shasta. During the process of driving, my car broke down. Really broke down, as in transmission went out, in the first three hours of our trip. We had the car towed, rented a car and continued on with the plans. We had a great trip.

Were there challenging moments? Yes, there were for me as I figured out how to be the third person in the group and found myself with two people who somehow forgot to say the word, 'thank you'. But I purposed to forgive and love them.

I had to keep a short account with my heart and forgive many times. I knew that if I did not forgive within moments of feeling hurt or not appreciated, I was quickly going to be picking up speed toward being resentful, bitter and angry. When they would whisper to each other, I would forgive them. When they would only talk to each other, I would forgive them. Not out loud, but within myself. Many, many times I forgave, situation after situation.

At the end of the trip, still no thank you. Yes, the enemy wanted me to get upset and say something. He knew better than that. I taught my son to be grateful. His sister is very grateful; what happened? Again, I would forgive. I tried very hard not to remind him to say thank you, as we moms do, at times (smile). If we are not mindful of this, we can actually step into the nagging category in wanting a thank you. I held my tongue. I forgave every time I wanted to hear the word thank you.

My final exam on forgiving came the night he was packing up and I found, on the table, his yearly Christmas letter which I write to him and each person in my family, letting them know how proud I am of them, what areas I have watched them grow in, and how much I love them. I asked him if he was going to pack it and his reply was, "I do not know what to do with it." I stood there as he told me this from the other room. I admit, I was a bit crushed and so hurt that it appeared to mean nothing to him, and he wasn't even going to hide the fact that he didn't want it. I purposed inside of me to choose to forgive him right there on the spot. I knew if I did not start forgiving him, I was going to start crying and tell him a thing or two. I forgave because I needed the Lord's help not to be hurt or offended.

After he left, I worked on my heart with the Lord, forgiving some more, as I never did hear that 'thank you', even as we said good-bye at the airport (I did from his girlfriend). I heard the Lord tell me the only reason I wanted to hear him say thank you was to get his approval of all I felt I did for him. He was right. I repented.

Over the next few days, the Lord showed me that his actions were communicating gratitude as he called many times and took care of things immediately when he got back to his home. He was grateful. He just showed it in a way that I did not notice as appreciation. I was shocked. I would never have seen it this way before, and certainly would not have if I had not worked on my heart and forgave. I learned a valuable lesson about myself. Gratitude comes in many forms, not just in words...

CHAPTER 14
Hand It Over

That moment when you get in the car after a hard conversation, or you hang up the phone from hearing things you did not want to hear. Or that moment you found out someone had lied to you or cheated on you...what do you do afterward? Do you want to call a friend or talk to your spouse? Do you want to post something on Facebook about them? You are angry, hurt, upset, disappointed, and you need to get it out, but how do you do it?

I was faced with this not long ago. I actually seem to face this type of situation often. I had a choice in what to do with the "after" part of the situation. The Lord has made me more aware of this choice. I usually want to call my daughter or my husband, but then, they have to deal with the hurt and get upset with the person or situation. So, I decided this one time to say nothing to anyone. I realized, in that moment, it was gossip when I run to other people first. Yes, we have figured out a way to rationalize it and justify it, but it is gossip. We want to tell someone because we want them to tell us how unfair it was, and how they were wrong and we were right. We want them to connect with the hurt and join our side.

Who wins in this situation? The enemy loves it when we immediately call someone to tell them about what happened. I can just see him smiling and rubbing his hands together in great satisfaction over how fast things can get blown up, and he does not have to do anything but watch. But what would love do?

What would happen if Jesus was the first person we talked to? He knows everything that just happened. He knows why it happened, and He also knows the solution. But if we were really honest, in the moment we get hurt, we do not want to hear truth, we want someone to hear us and agree with us. I chose to talk to Him about it first. I told Him I was hurt, and how dare they do that or say that. I went on and on until it was out of my system. Then I apologized and asked Him to forgive me and to help me understand. I was, then, thinking clearly. The next day, when I talked to people I was calm and gave very little detail, and gave the information from the side of resolved inside. The people I tell do not have to deal with any issues rising up inside of them to protect me. The issue is no longer an issue. Interesting how that works...Love does not create additional issues for other people...

A few days later, I kept thinking about the word 'submit'. This is not a favorite word most people like to hear, but I listened. I thought about the Scripture in James 4:7, "Therefore submit to God. Resist the devil and he will flee from you." As I thought about it, He showed me a different way to see the word 'submit'. What if it is like when we are asked to submit a form to an organization or company? I saw it as the Lord asking us to hand it to Him, submit, and let Him take care of it. When I applied this verse to the many situations I encounter, I gained understanding in a whole new freeing way. I hand the person or situation to Him. By doing this, I am resisting the temptation the enemy is trying to tempt me with in calling or telling someone what happened. Resisting happens when we submit it or hand it to Him. He takes it and covers it with His love...

It seems simple. It is becoming my first choice, and I find myself handing many people and situations to Him. Things that are out of my control and are tempting me to worry about them, I am submitting them to Him. I literally hand it to Him. All of the worry lifts. This is applied with anything that is bringing anxiety, hurt, concern, worry, pain, harm, fear, and anything else...submit it to God. Tell Him about it, He knows what to do, and the best part, He will not tell anyone...devil flees... love wins!

CHAPTER 15
A Hug

May I give you a hug? No, was my reply to this question years ago. I was hardened and trusted very few people. I was filled with unforgiveness even though I was a Christian and went to church. Life was a bit tough on me and my response was to withdraw. I would hug, but close family was really all I was willing to embrace. I'm not sure what people at church thought when I told them no, but I really did not care, either.

When I had my daughter at age 27, I birthed love with her. I was so in love with her. I did not really know that it was possible to feel this way. Her birth started something in me. I had my son at age 33, and again, love was birthed with him as well. The love they needed came with them.

But I was still quite closed off to hugs with other people. Maybe a short token hug, as I would call it. You know, the type where you sort of put your arms around the other person and tap them on the back and quickly pull away, or the courtesy side hugs of very limited contact. Yes, I was one of those. They were safe, and, I guess, the other person was fine with it. I never really asked, and I was always relieved when that part of a greeting was over.

But, thirteen years ago, at the age of 40, I had a radical encounter with the Holy Spirit of God, and much of that hardness began to melt away. I encountered His love for me and my life was forever changed. He hugged me that night on February 5th, and I hugged Him back.

My journey with hugging has changed. As I have worked on my heart and on forgiving, I have opened myself up to more of Him. As I experience more of Him, I discover that I have something to give. When I hug people now, I actually feel love pour out of me. I now love to hug. I am not talking about sexual hugs, but secure hugs. I give a hug that tells the other person God is with them. I give a hug that tells them everything is going to be okay. I give a hug that brings safety and comfort to the one in need of it. I give a hug that communicates help, hope, and the love of Jesus to those in need.

When I hug now, people usually say, "You are a good hugger." I always smile inside, because I know Who is hugging through me, and I also know who I used to be. When I hug people, I release peace, I release healing, I allow Jesus to occupy me and hug them. I am amazed at how many times a hug can change everything for a person. I love to hug. My hugs are intended to release Jesus, and people have come to know that.

A HUG

I give momma hugs. I give friend hugs. I give hugs of comfort, security, and peace. I can usually tell how a person is doing when I hug them. I usually do not let go until I feel them receive His love through me. I do not know how else to explain it, but I have gone up to women (not men) that I do not know in church and asked them if I can hug them. I know when the Lord wants to give someone a hug. For me, when I have nothing to say, a hug is best.

Yes, I encounter people who are like I used to be and I hug them stronger. At times, the hugs are awkward when the other person is not comfortable with a good long hug, but after the hug, they are usually peaceful and left wondering what in the world just happened. I want them to experience the love of God through me...

Where are you in the process of hugging? I went from stay away to hugging is my first choice. Only God! I am given to love, and sometimes that love comes in the form of a big long hug from God! When I hug, I mean it. I pray that as you read this, you, too, will experience a hug from heaven...

John 13:34-35 & John 15:12-14

CHAPTER 16
His Commandment

I thought this book was complete until I read John chapters 13 and 15. You might want to get your Bible and read those chapters. These are the last moments of Jesus' life here on earth. He knows He is going to be captured, tortured, and hung on a cross to die. He also knows He is going to be victorious over death. He knows what is going to happen to His disciples when all of this begins, so the words He is speaking are even more important. Think about it, if you knew you were going to die very soon, you would want to make some important points that you did not want those you love to forget. Read those chapters from that perspective and importance. So, what were the most important things Jesus wanted His disciples to know?

He starts out with washing their feet. We can tell by Peter's response that they are not comfortable with this. They know who He is. What would you do if Jesus wanted to wash your feet? Is this Jesus modeling love?

Judas, then, leaves the scene to go and fulfill Scripture and betray Jesus. Now, Jesus is alone with just the eleven disciples. When He is alone He gives them a new commandment in verse 34 and 35 of chapter 13, "A new commandment I give to you, that you love one another; as I have loved you, that you also love one another. By this all will know that you are My disciples, if you have love for one another." Stop for a moment and read those two verses again. They are important. We had the Ten Commandments, and then the two in Mark 12:30-31, which were a response to the scribes questions, and now, Jesus Himself is handing us a new commandment. Love one another as I have loved you. He is telling them, and us, that this is how the world will know we are His disciples. This is how the world will know Jesus, by our love for one another. Think about that...

In chapter 15 of John, Jesus brings it even closer to the eleven disciples in verses 12-14, "This is My commandment, that you love one another as I have loved you. Greater love has no one than this, than to lay down one's life for his friends. You are My friends if you do whatever I command you." This is not a new commandment anymore, but His. He is preparing them for His death, and communicating that His death is for love. He laid down His life for them. They still did not really know what was going to happen, but when He died, these words, most likely, hit home. We know the entire story, but they did not. Now, receive His words as words being spoken directly to you. You be the 'you' in these verses. Just you and Jesus...

HIS COMMANDMENT

He was given in love, to love, and modeled love for us, so that we can love one another as He loved us. I hope this book has stirred you to choose to be given to love in new ways. Here are some questions to dig deeper into this...

1. What are these verses saying to you?

2. What are you going to do about it?

3. How are we in the Body of Christ doing with His commandment? How are you doing with it? Sit with the Lord and allow Him to search your heart...

4. Think about the 10 commandments, the first two, and then those here in this chapter. What is the relevance to you?

CHAPTER 17
So Love Is

So love is...

learning...
changing...
being still and knowing He is God...
determination and a purposed choice...
listening...
suffers long and is kind...
does not envy...
does not parade itself...
is not puffed up...
does not behave rudely...
does not seek its own...
is not provoked...
thinks no evil...

does not rejoice in iniquity...
rejoices in the truth...
bears all things...
believes all things...
hopes all things...
endures all things and never fails...
relationship...
the 10 commandments...
loving others as we love ourselves...
developing a heart that receives God's love and gives it...
being secure in His love for us...
taking care of someone you love...
speaking truth in love...
supporting and being there...
giving your life and allowing love to be birthed in another person from you...
forgiving...
not avoiding...
does not create additional issues for other people...
a hug...
loving as He loved...

All of this is possible with God. He made us to love...this list is our potential and part of our DNA...

I pray with the Apostle Paul for you from Ephesians 3:14-21...

For this reason I bow my knees to the Father of our Lord Jesus Christ, from whom the whole family in heaven and earth is named, that He would grant you, according to the riches of His glory, to be strengthened with might through His Spirit in the inner man, that Christ may dwell in your hearts through faith; that you, being rooted and grounded in love, may be able to comprehend with all the saints what is the width and length and depth and height — to know the love of Christ which passes knowledge; that you may be filled with all fullness of God. Now to Him who is able to do exceedingly abundantly above all that we ask or think, according to the power that works in us, to Him be glory in the church by Christ Jesus to all generations, forever and ever. Amen

Do You Need Jesus?

If, for some reason, you have received this book and you do not know Jesus as your personal Savior, I want you to know that you can. Are you curious about this love I am talking about in this book? Do you want to experience it so that you can give it? If yes, then I want you to know that there is nothing you have done that He will not forgive, if you ask Him. Just say this simple prayer to begin your amazing journey with Jesus...

Dear Jesus,

Thank You for loving me and for dying on the cross for me. I ask that You please forgive me of my sins and that You come into my heart. I need You and want to get to know You. I want the love You came to give. Show me who You are. I want to love You.

In Jesus' name. Amen.

It is that simple.
Welcome to the family of God!

May I encourage you to please get connected with a local church family that will help you learn more about what you have just done. If you do not know of one, please contact me and I will help you find one.

About the Author

Cheryl Stasinowsky is a speaker and writer of passion and transparency. Her desire is for others to see Jesus in everything they walk through; growing a new passion for His Word and its relevance for them. Please contact her to make arrangements for your future events, retreats, church services, meetings, and conferences.

She would love to meet you!

cheryl@wordscribeministries.com
www.wordscribeministries.com
www.hishiddentreasure.blogspot.com

Connect with Cheryl on Facebook and twitter
@histreasures

What others are saying:

"Cheryl Stasinowsky is a treasure. Cheryl is a special artist that paints her teachings in faith constructionism, and as such, she passionately extracts the blueprints from the foundation of the Word and then builds that foundation into the details of everyday practical life. Her books and teachings are a life guide, and her speaking appearances are personal. She opens herself to each person she is teaching, and lays out in honesty her own personal experiences of the presence of God within the joys and pains of everyday life."

More Titles by Cheryl Stasinowsky

His Hidden Treasures
ISBN: 978-0-6158979-9-8

There is an unknown treasure sitting on your night stand, bookshelf or coffee table. It is full of keys that will unlock your destiny, vision and purpose. They are yours for the taking. Join Cheryl on this journey as she uncovers valuable secrets found in the Bible. Through her own brokenness and surrender, the author will inspire you to embark on your own journey of searching for the timeless and endless treasures in the Word of God. As you dig deeper, each hidden treasure will leave you desperate for more of God's Word.

Deeper Relevance
ISBN: 978-0-6159069-9-7

Cheryl set out to write a daily encouraging word on her social networks, not realizing that her pursuit for a deeper understanding of God's Word would blossom into a full devotional. Grab your Bible, along with this book, and get ready to discover kingdom nuggets that will enrich your walk and relationship with Jesus. His Word truly sustains us every day!

More Titles by Cheryl Stasinowsky

Now Faith
ISBN: 978-0-615899-07-7

Now Faith is a face-to-face encounter with the men and women of Hebrews 11 who had the kind of faith that pleased God and moved mountains. Each chapter steps inside their lives, takes a look around, finds vital parts of the DNA of their faith, and then supplies a prayer for the impartation of that faith.

Now Faith in Spanish (Es Pues, La Fe)
ISBN: 978-0-615899-67-1

Es Pues, La Fe es un encuentro, cara a cara, con los hombres y mujeres de Hebreos 11 quienes tuvieron la fe que agradó a Dios y que movió montañas. Cada capítulo toma un paso adentro de sus vidas, echa un vistazo a su forma de ser, encuentra partes vitales del ADN de su fe, y después suple una oración para la impartición de esa fe.

More Titles by Cheryl Stasinowsky

Private Moments With God
ISBN: 978-0-6159103-7-6

Life as we individually know it ... Each of us has a past that is influencing how we see our present. We walk through our day with all of the pressures and demands of life with a past, in the present, and also with a hope for a future. I, too, journey this thing called life. Through it all, I have come to value to the highest degree the first moments of my early mornings when the house is quiet, it is still dark outside, my coffee is freshly brewed, my iPod is playing worship music in my ears, and I open the Word of God for my nourishment and encouragement for the day. These are those moments ...

Given to Forgive
ISBN: 978-0-692306-60-4

Are you tired of wrestling with regret, guilt, anger, resentment, bitterness, and impatience? Did you know that all of these are symptoms of unforgiveness? I did not like to forgive and always thought that the other person had to come to me first to apologize. I held onto unforgiveness for years. Eight years ago, I started forgiving people, situations, and choices I had made. I hand you my journey of choosing to be given to forgive every day...

More Titles by Cheryl Stasinowsky

Given to Prayer
ISBN: 978-0-692629-68-0

This is not a book on formulas to pray better. This is a book filled with my own personal journey in learning how He communicates with me. I share thoughts, struggles, victories, and defeats. I do not profess to have prayer all figured out. I think it is a life-long discovery for each individual..

Coming soon ...

GIVEN TO CHANGE

GIVEN TO LISTEN

All of Cheryl's books are available in
eBook and print versions on Amazon and Barnes & Noble.

www.ingramcontent.com/pod-product-compliance
Lightning Source LLC
Chambersburg PA
CBHW071519040426
42444CB00008B/1717